I Love Po...

At the Show

Sandy Ransford

D0510043

Editor: Amanda Askew
Designer: Izzy Langridge

Copyright © QED Publishing 2011

First published in the UK in 2011 by
QED Publishing
A Quarto Group company
226 City Road
London EC1V 2TT

www.qed-publishing.co.uk

A catalogue record for this book is available from the British Library.

ISBN 978 1 84835 659 7

Printed in China

Website information is correct at time of going to press. The publishers cannot accept liability for the content of the Internet sites that you visit, nor for any information or links found on third-party websites.

Picture credits
(t=top, b=bottom, l=left, r=right, c=centre, fc=front cover)

All images are courtesy of Bob Langrish images unless stated below.
Alamy 2br Rex Moreton, 9tr PCJones, 9bl The Photolibrary Wales
DK Images 4r John Henderson, 5br Andy Crawford, 6r Bob Langrish, 7br Andy Crawford, 15b Dorling Kindersley,
Dreamstime 2mr Harperdrewart,
Shutterstock 3br Groomee, nito

Words in **bold** are explained in the Glossary on page 22.

Remember!
Children must always wear appropriate clothing, including a riding hat, and follow safety guidelines when handling or riding horses and ponies.

Contents

Preparing your pony

At the show 4

Leading-rein class 6

First Ridden and Showing classes 8

Working Hunter Pony classes 10

Gymkhana races 12

Handy Pony class 14

Fancy Dress class 16

Dressage and eventing 18

Glossary 20

Index 22

Notes for parents and teachers 23

24

Preparing your pony

When you enter your pony in a competition, it must look its best – clean and well groomed – to help you and your pony get the top prize.

Grooming

To get your pony's coat gleaming, you need to groom it well with a **body brush**. Then give it a final polish with the stable rubber to remove dust and loose hairs.

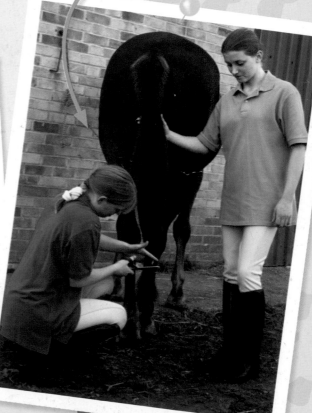

Quarter marks

Patterns made on the pony's quarters using comb, or a stencil and a damp water brush, are called quarter marks. Brush or comb the hair in different directions to create the effect.

Plaiting the mane and tail

You can plait the top of the tail to make it look neat. Manes are divided into sections, which are plaited, folded under and sewn into place.

Top tip!

It is easier to plait the mane if you dampen the sections first.

You should look after your pony's tack well, so that it lasts a long time.

Cleaning the tack

Clean the tack (the saddle and bridle) every time you use it, and give it a good clean before a competition. Rub saddle soap into the leather with a damp sponge until the tack is soft. Wash the bit and stirrup irons carefully to get rid of all the dirt, then rub them dry until they gleam.

At the show

If you are going to ride in a show, make sure that you look as neat and clean as your pony. When you're at a show, rest your pony between classes. Let it graze, and give it a drink of water.

hard hat

stock

gloves

riding jacket

jodhpurs

riding boots

Riding clothes
At a show, you need to wear proper riding clothes – jodhpurs with riding boots, a shirt and tie, a riding jacket, gloves and your hard hat. Your clothes should be clean and tidy, and your boots must be well polished.

If you are competing in jumping classes, you will need to wear a body protector. This protects your back from injury in case you fall off.

Arriving

Try to arrive at a show with plenty of time to spare. Collect your number from the secretary's tent and check that both you and your pony look clean and tidy. Listen for your class to be called over the public address system.

If you're in a jumping class, you will be able to jump over a few practice fences while you wait.

In the collecting ring

The collecting ring is a small ring near the entrance to the main ring, where competitors wait until it is time for their class. You may want to practise your trot and canter, but don't work the pony too hard. You don't want it to be sweating when you go in the ring.

Leading-rein class

If you are young and new to riding, your first **showing** class may well be on a leading-rein. A parent or another adult will lead the pony round while you ride as well as you can.

Correct dress

In a leading-rein class, the handler has to wear the right clothes as well as the rider. For men, this is a suit, a tie, gloves and a hat; for women, this is a skirt, jacket, hat and gloves.

This pony, its rider and handler all look very smart.

In the ring

The leading-rein competitors walk, then trot, around the ring together. The judge then calls them in to line up, and each does an **individual show**, such as trotting a circle in each direction.

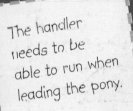

The handler needs to be able to run when leading the pony.

Choosing the winner

When everyone has done their show, the ponies walk round again. Then, they line up in winning order – first, second, third, and so on. The first four or five receive a rosette.

First Ridden and Showing classes

Many shows have a First Ridden class for young riders who are competing in a show for the first time off the leading-rein.

First Ridden classes

These classes are for young riders, but this time you ride on your own. The ponies go round together in both walk and trot, and then line up, as in the leading-rein class. The judge examines the ponies one at a time, and you each do an individual show. In this class you may canter, as well as walk and trot, in your show.

walk

trot

canter

Categories of Showing class	
Height	Rider age
Up to 12. 2 hh (128 cm)	Up to 13 years
12. 2 hh to 13.2 hh (138 cm)	Up to 15 years
13.2 hh to 14.2 hh (148 cm)	Up to 17 years

Showing classes

Similar to the First Ridden, the Showing classes allow you to canter round the ring together, as well as walk and trot. You will also have to dismount, remove your pony's saddle, and walk and trot it out to show the judge how well your pony moves.

The height of a horse or pony is measured in hands. One hand is equal to 10.16 centimetres.

Leading an unridden horse or pony round a show ring is called showing **in-hand**.

Winning a rosette

If you win a rosette, the judge fastens it to the pony's bridle, or to the string of your number. You will canter round the ring in a lap of honour, in the order of judging. When the spectators clap, be sure you have control of your pony, or it may get over-excited.

Working Hunter Pony classes

These classes combine the skills needed for both Showing classes and show jumping.

In the ring

A Working Hunter Pony is expected to do all the things a show pony does, as well as gallop and jump. In Phase One, each competitor goes round the jumping course in turn. In Phase Two, the whole class goes round the ring together in walk, trot and canter. Finally, the ponies gallop round the ring one at a time.

It's showtime!
A score is given for each phase. The scores are added together to find the winner.

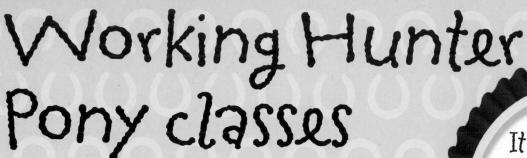

The course might include fences such as these rails. The jumps won't be too high.

Show jumping

This sport involves riding round a course and jumping many different types of fence. The fences are coloured and have different distances between them.

Preparing to jump

You can walk round a show-jumping course before the class and work out how many strides you need to take when approaching each fence. The fences are numbered to help you know your way round. Competitors jump the course one at a time.

The scoring system

Each competitor collects **faults** for knocking down fences, refusing to jump them, missing one out and going over the time limit. The rider with the smallest number of faults wins.

Types of fence

Show-jumping rings contain spread-fences such as an oxer, and uprights such as a wall. The 'bricks' are wooden blocks that are easy to knock down without injuring the pony.

Oxer

Crossed rails

Wall

Gymkhana races

Entering gymkhana classes is lots of fun. Many of them are races, and you need a speedy pony that will turn and stop when and where you want it to. It is useful to be able to vault onto your pony to save time.

With lots of practice, you can vault onto a pony while it's moving.

Bending race
This race needs a well-trained pony. You have to weave your way along a line of upright poles, turn at the end, then weave your way back again.

Potato race

In this race, you have to pick up a potato, gallop down the field and then put it in a bucket. You then go back for the next potato, and the person who gets all their potatoes in the bucket first is the winner.

Sack race

In this race, you canter down the field, get off your pony and climb into a sack. Then, leading your pony, you get back to the start as fast as you can. Most people jump along, holding the pony with one hand and the sack with the other.

Egg-and-spoon race

Carrying an egg on a spoon while running as fast as you can and leading your pony is not easy. The eggs aren't real ones, but if you do drop one, you have to stop and pick it up again.

Handy Pony class

For the Handy Pony class, you need an obedient, calm, well-behaved pony. In this class, you have to do all kinds of unusual tasks while riding your pony.

A task may involve walking or trotting over a number of poles laid on the ground.

Your pony needs to be well behaved while you jump and lead it at the same time as walking along a row of upturned tubs.

You might have to dismount, pick something up, then mount again and take the object to another part of the ring.

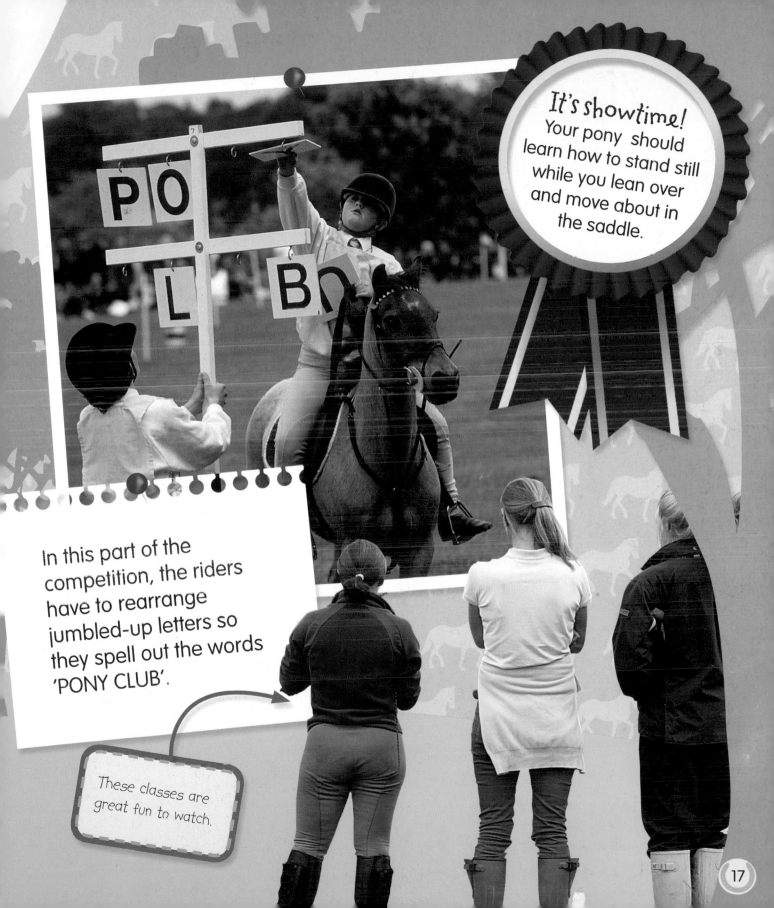

It's showtime! Your pony should learn how to stand still while you lean over and move about in the saddle.

In this part of the competition, the riders have to rearrange jumbled-up letters so they spell out the words 'PONY CLUB'.

These classes are great fun to watch.

Fancy Dress class

This is lots of fun! In a Fancy Dress class, you and your pony dress up. You are characters, so you need to plan the costume, and you may need some help in making it. The best costume wins.

Spots before your eyes
This rider has made her pony match her costume by painting spots on it. If you do this, only use washable water-soluble paint so you can wash it off again.

This young rider has used pink paint on the pony's mane and tail and given it a paper horn to look like a unicorn!

It's herding time!

To make yourself look like a cowboy or cowgirl, wear chaps over your jodhpurs, a shirt and waistcoat, tie a neckerchief round your neck, and fit a Stetson-type hat over your riding hat. Tie a roll of rope to your saddle, and ride your pony with the reins held in one hand.

You could wear a Santa suit or an elf costume. Then turn your pony into Rudolph, the red-nosed reindeer.

Rudolph costume

Fix fake antlers to your pony's bridle and paint its nose red with water-soluble paint. Then twist tinsel around the bridle, draping it over the pony's neck.

Dressage and eventing

Dressage and eventing are competitions for experienced riders. In dressage your pony has to perform precise movements and paces.

The dressage arena
A dressage arena has a low fence round it and letters along the sides. Most arenas measure 40 metres by 20 metres, but for some international competitions, they are 60 metres by 20 metres.

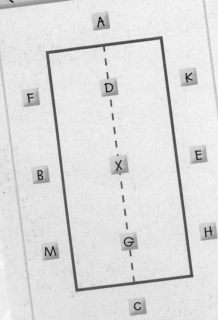

Markers around an arena (40 metres by 20 metres)

You have to learn the test first – although in some **novice** tests, it may be read out to you. For example, you might walk into the arena at A, trot to C, canter from C to F, walk from F to E, and so on.

Advanced tasks include changes of leg at every stride in canter, pirouettes and piaffe – a sort of slow trotting on the spot.

Eventing

This sport involves dressage, cross-country and show-jumping. In the cross-country section, you ride a course of difficult jumps within a set time. The course usually involves jumping into and out of a lake.

Cross-country

To ride 'cross-country' means galloping over a course of jumps set out in parkland. You have to be an experienced rider, with a bold, brave horse or pony.

Hunter trials

These are jumping competitions ridden across fields and through woods, for both horses and ponies. You may also have to open and close gates. There is usually a set time in which the course has to be completed.

Glossary

Body brush A short-bristled brush used for removing dirt and grease from a pony's coat.

Dressage A competition in which a horse or pony has to carry out precise actions and paces.

Faults Penalty points gained in jumping competitions.

Fetlocks The lowest joints in a horse's or pony's legs, just above the hooves.

Individual show A display of your pony's action and paces, carried out in a showing class.

In-hand Leading an unridden horse or pony while on foot.

Novice A pony or rider that is inexperienced in what it is doing.

Showing Exhibiting a horse or pony at a show, where it is judged on its obedience, paces and behaviour.

Index

arriving at the show 7

bending race 14
body brush 4, 22
body protector 6

clothes 2, 6, 8
collecting ring 7
costumes 18–19
cross-country 21

dressage 20, 21, 22
    arena 20

egg-and-spoon race 15
eventing 21

Fancy dress class 18–19
faults 13, 22
fences 12, 13
fetlocks 4, 22
First Ridden class 10

grooming 4
gymkhana races 14–15

handlers 8, 9
hands (measurement) 11
Handy pony class 16–17
height 11
hunter trials 21

individual shows 9, 10, 22

lap of honour 11
Leading-rein class 8–9

mane 5

novices 20, 22

piaffe 20
pirouettes 20
poles 16
potato race 15
preparing your pony 4–5

quarter marks 4

resting your pony 6
rosettes 9, 11

sack race 15
saddle soap 5
safety 2, 6
show-jumping 7, 12, 13, 21
Showing classes 11
showing in-hand 11

tack, cleaning 5
tail,
    plaiting 5
    trimming 4

vaulting 14

Working hunter
    pony classes 12–13

Notes for parents and teachers

All shows, gymkhanas and competitions have sets of rules that have to be adhered to. If you are new to competing, you should familiarize yourself with them before entering. Make sure the rider is wearing the correct form of riding clothes, and that they understand what entering the class involves.

Whatever kind of class the child enters, make sure that they practise with the pony as much as possible, so by the time of the competition, they both know exactly what they are doing. It's best to keep an individual show simple, but to carry out each pace and change of pace as well as possible. Teach the pony to do a good, square halt, with both forefeet and both hind feet in line with each other, and make sure the pony will stand until told to move on again.

Encourage the child to watch other classes, to see how the ponies perform and how well the riders ride them. If a pony is particularly well schooled, see if the child can work out exactly what the rider does to get it to move so well.

When watching jumping classes, point out how many strides different ponies take on approaching a fence. Ask the child to imagine how many strides they would need to take on their pony.

It's fun to construct miniature show jumps at home. Pencils can be painted to make poles, matchboxes to make walls, and small twigs between two pencils tied together with string will make a brush fence. Even if children ride ponies, they will enjoy playing with toy ponies and jumps on a rainy day.

Horse and pony websites

www.bef.co.uk
British Equestrian Federation

www.bhs.org.uk
British Horse Society

www.pcuk.org
The Pony Club

www.horsesport.org
Fédération Equestre Internationale (the international body that regulates equestrian sport)

www.worldhorsewelfare.org
World Horse Welfare